JESTIFIED

WORDS

JEST FOR FUN

WAYNE G.HAVINS

I would like to dedicate this book to my Mom,
Kathy Langan who put up with me,
My Sister Tai Hegenbart and Her husband
Eric for their support and encouragement,
and in memory of my dear friend Larry
McGuinnigle for his support and his laughs,
who was the inspiration for this book.
Thanks you guys
Wayne

PRINTED IN THE UNITED STATES OF AMERICA
PUBLISHED BY BOOKMARKETEERS.COM

What TV Program is always napping?

WHERE DO ALASKANS
STAY WHEN THEY
TRAVEL?

AT AN ESKAMOTEL

How does a Gorilla
start his car?

With a MonKEY

A BALLerina

What kind of Ball dances?

WHAT ANIMAL FLOATS
DOWN THE RIVER?

A GIRAFFTE

WHAT STATE IS BEST FOR SUNBATHING?

MONTANA

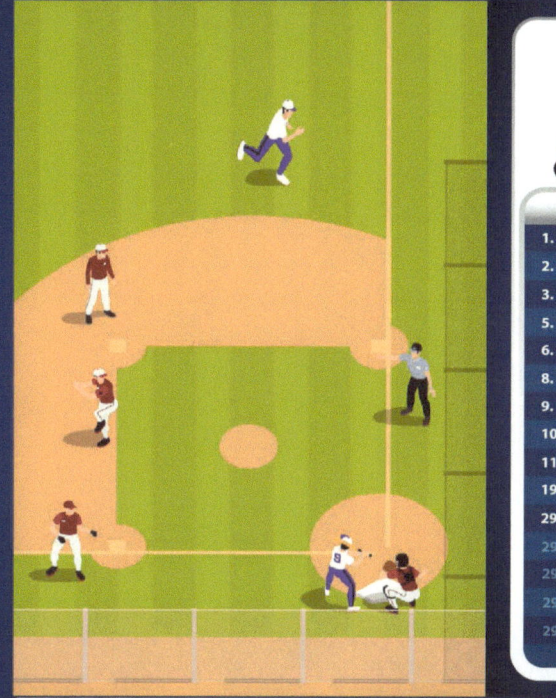

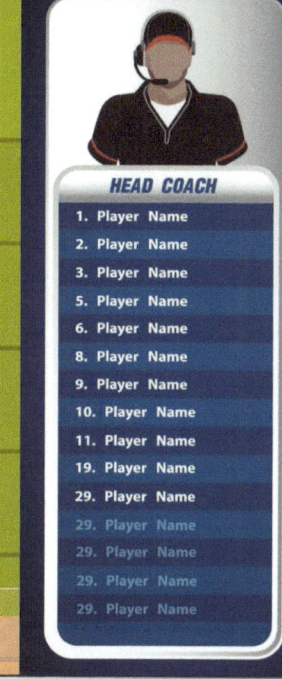

STADIUM NAME

STADIUM NAME

HEAD COACH

1. Player Name
2. Player Name
3. Player Name
5. Player Name
6. Player Name
8. Player Name
9. Player Name
10. Player Name
11. Player Name
19. Player Name
29. Player Name
29. Player Name
29. Player Name
29. Player Name
29. Player Name

HEAD COACH

1. Player Name
2. Player Name
3. Player Name
5. Player Name
6. Player Name
8. Player Name
9. Player Name
10. Player Name
11. Player Name
19. Player Name
29. Player Name
29. Player Name
29. Player Name
29. Player Name
29. Player Name

What Creature keeps baseball stats?

The SCOREpion

What do you call a pile of Monkeys?

An OrangaTANGLE

Where does a Knight park his Rescue Vehicle?

In an
AmbuLANCE A LOT

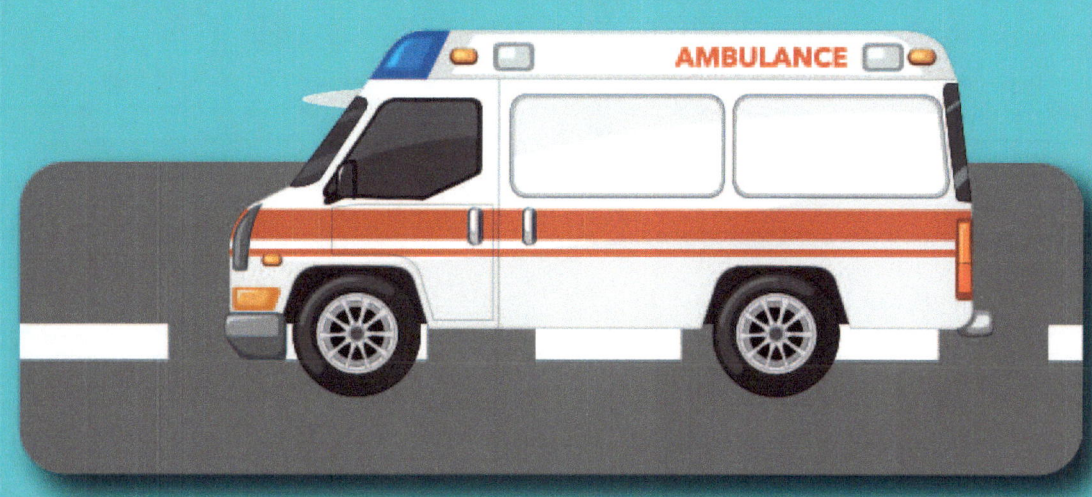

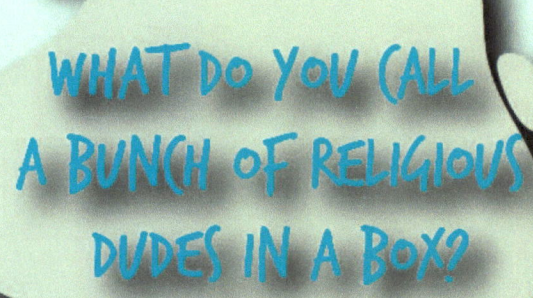

WHAT DO YOU CALL A BUNCH OF RELIGIOUS DUDES IN A BOX?

A DECK OF CARDINALS

What is a Rabbits towel called?

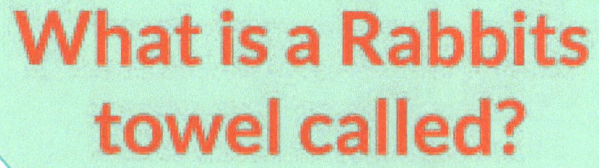

'A HARE DRYER'

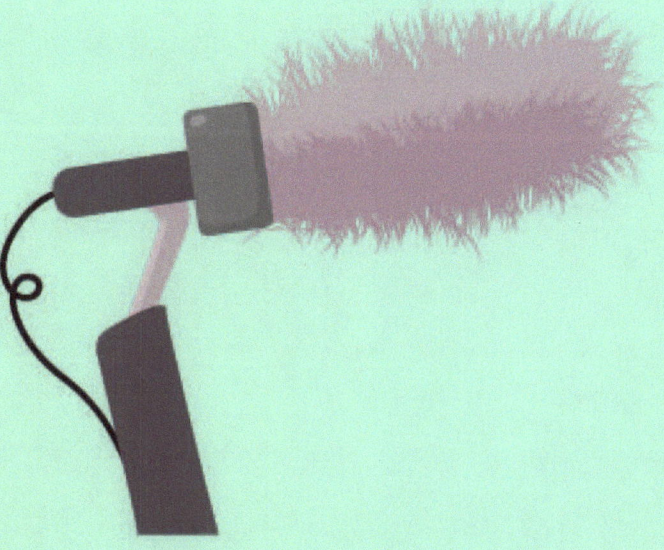

What State is Santas Favorite?

OklaHO-HO-HOma

What is a Bricklayers teacher called?

His ceMENTOR

What is a Ducks
favorite snack?

Ritz Quackers

What do you call a greedy Bunny?

gRABBIT

What kind of school
do planets attend?

A UNIVERSEity

What mountain sneezes?

A VolcaNOSE

What do you give a Red wood for being good

A TREEt

What Super Hero
serves Ice Cream?

SCOOPerMan

What State can you dance on?

FLOORida

What Brand of Coffee do Mountains prefer?

Hills Bros

WHAT FISH HAS THE MOST HORSEPOWER?

THE RACECARP

A BLIMPle

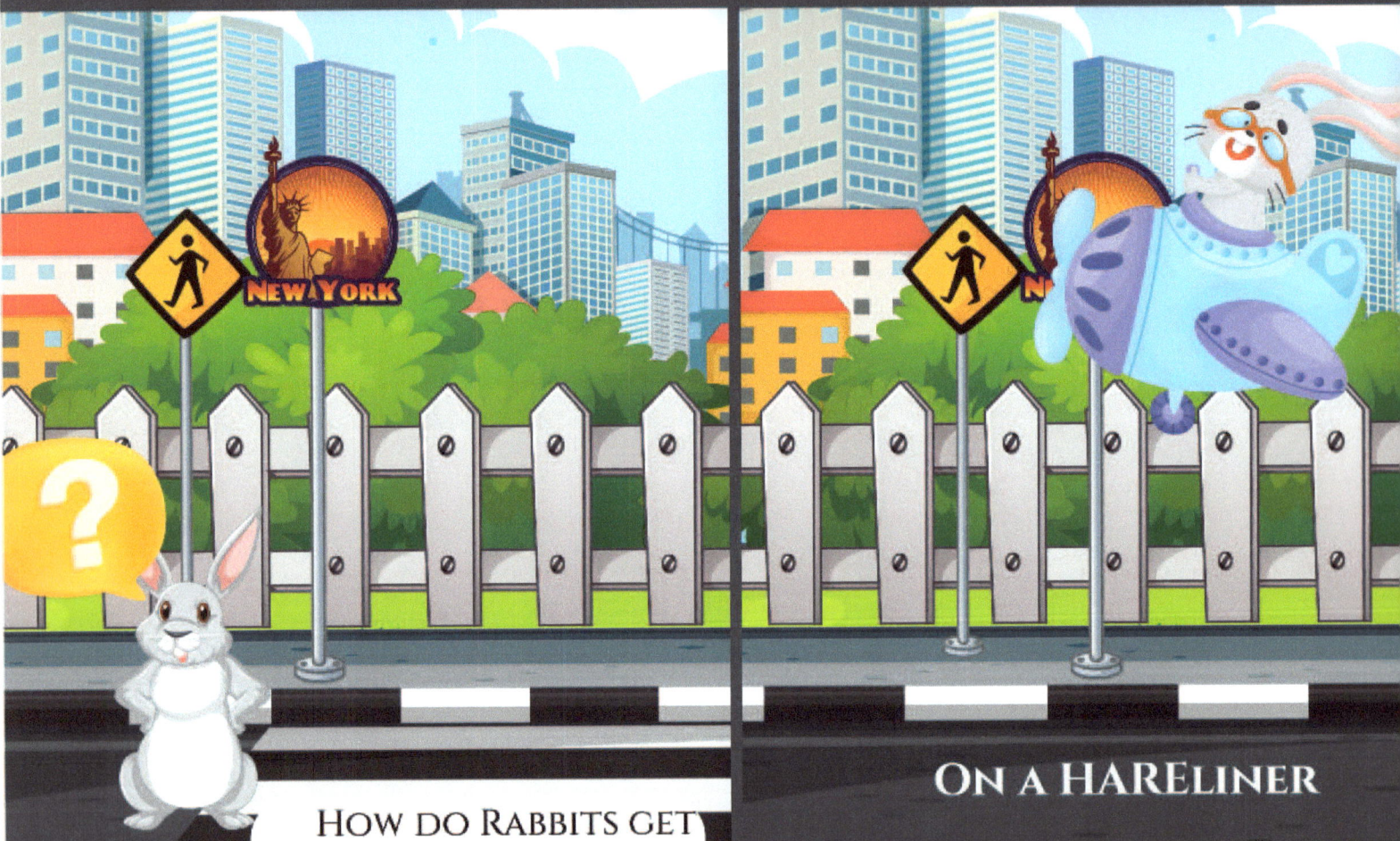

HOW DO RABBITS GET FROM L A TO NEW YORK?

ON A HARELINER

WHAT FRUIT HAS A BACKBONE?

THE SPINEAP[PLE]

WHERE DO YOU SEND CRAZY PLANETS?

What monkey is Puffed-up?

The BaBALOON

How do you cut the Ocean in half?

With a SEAsaw

A FULL OF BULLDOG

WHAT DOG IS ALWAYS TELLING STORIES ?

What kind of music does a Swamp listen to?

MARSH MELLOWROCK

What Fish has the hardest skull?

The STEELhead

WHAT DO YOU CALL A
FAKE HORSE?

A SHETLAND PHONY

It's BOARD

4

2

Why is the 2x4 not paying attention?

Where does trash go real fast ?

A Waste track

What Plant is a gymnist?

The TUMBLEweed

What Boat cuts wood and is also a State?

ARK an SAW

WHAT VAMPIRE DRIVES
A RACECAR?

COUNT DRAGULA

WHAT DO YOU CALL A BABY DUMPTRUCK?

A DUMPLING

What insect do Hikers prefer?

The WalkingSTICK

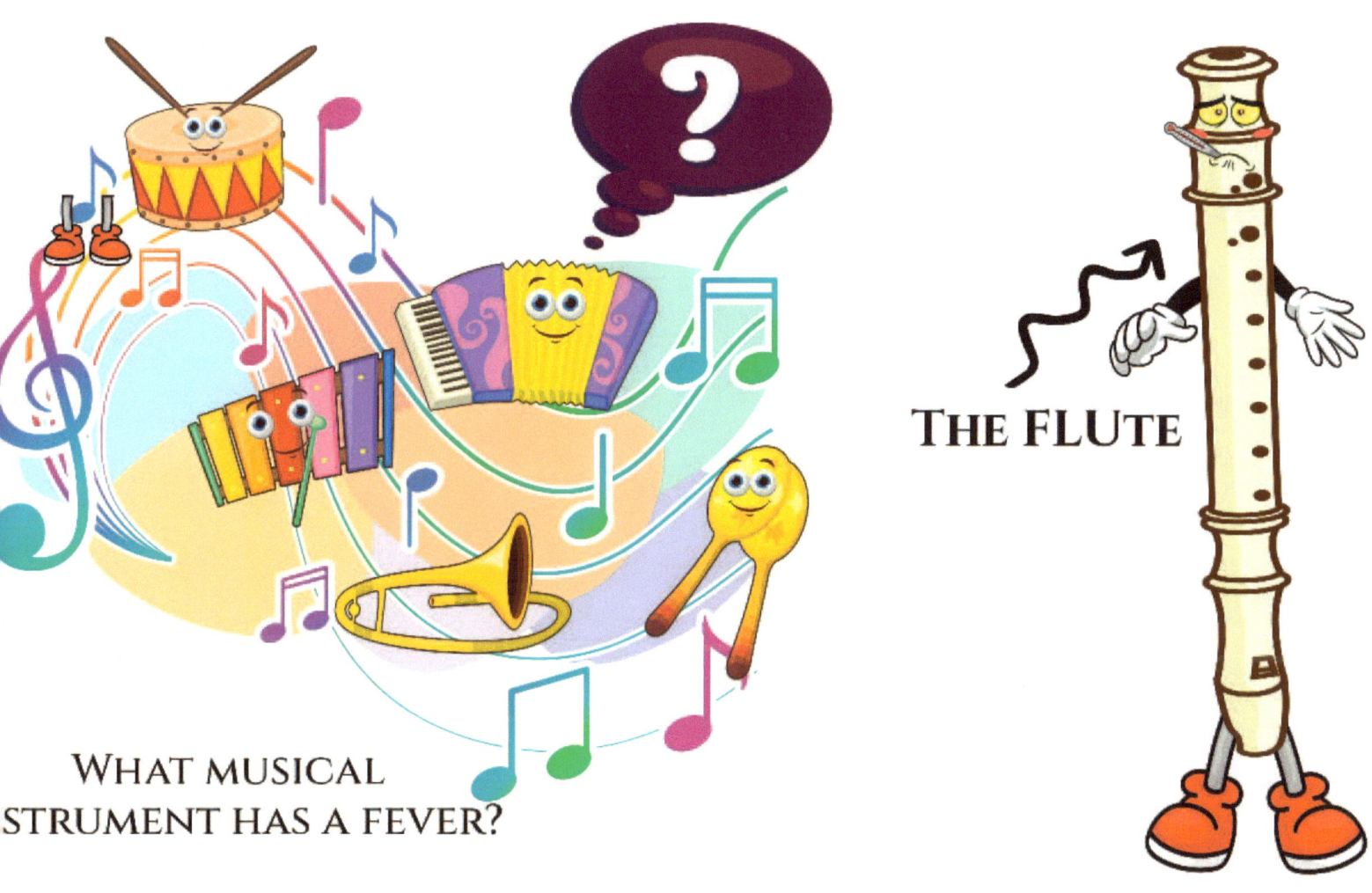

WHAT MUSICAL STRUMENT HAS A FEVER?

THE FLUTE

How many insects make a foot?

12 Inchworms

What insect can only be a girlfriend?

The LadyBug

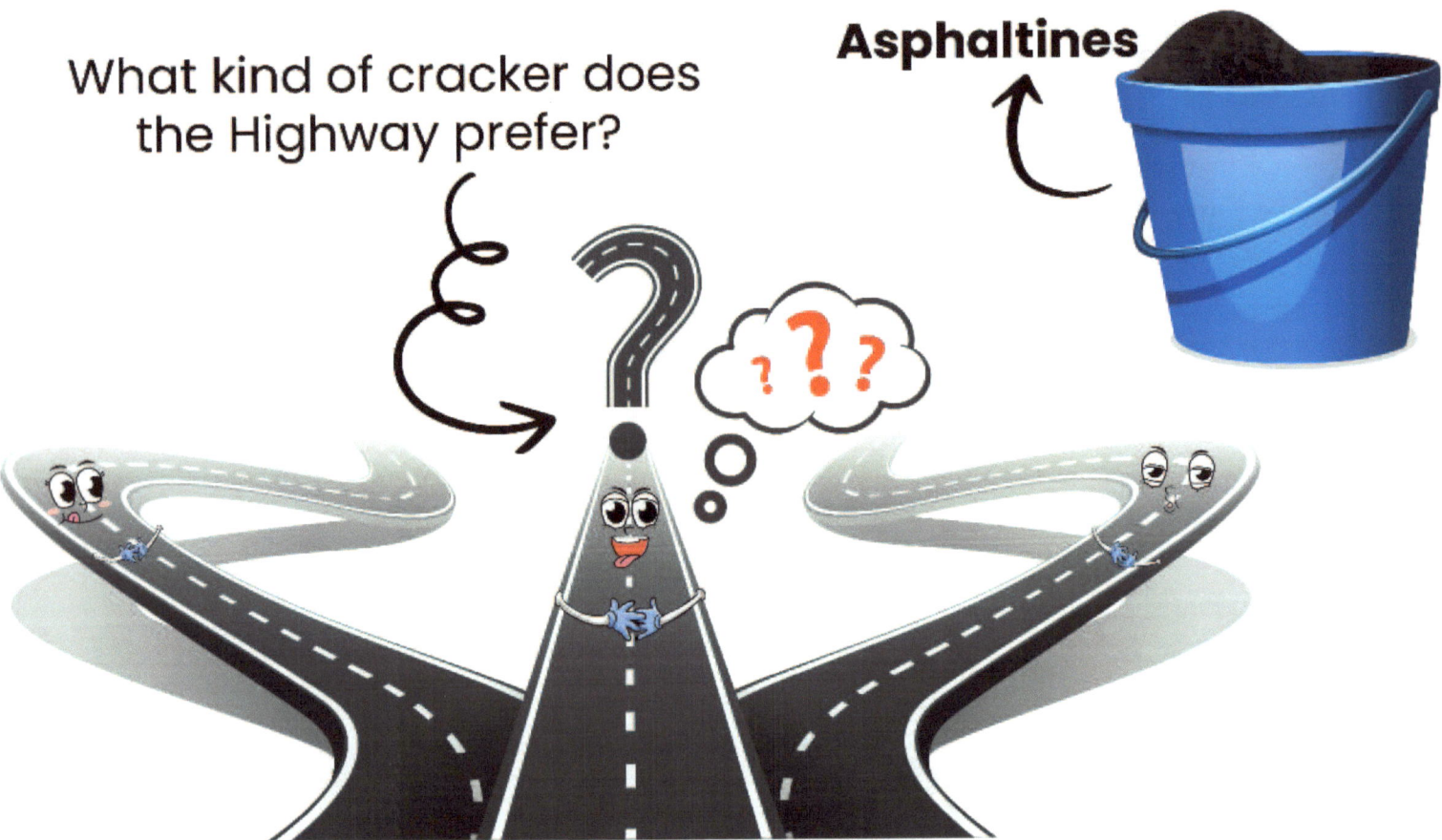

How do you heat up a Workout?

With an AroBIC lighter

WHAT VEGGIE NEEDS
THE HEIMLICH MANUVER?

AN ARTICHOKE

What do you call a
baby Skunk?

A little SQUIRT

Hair BUNS

What does a WIG snack on?

Where do sidewalks go when they die?

A CEMENTary

Why don't Eggs laugh?

They are afraid to
CRACKUP

What Dinasaur always crashes?

The T-Wrecks

What Reptile wrote a Cookbook?

Betty Crockerdial

WHAT SNAKE WEARS AN
UTILITY BELT?

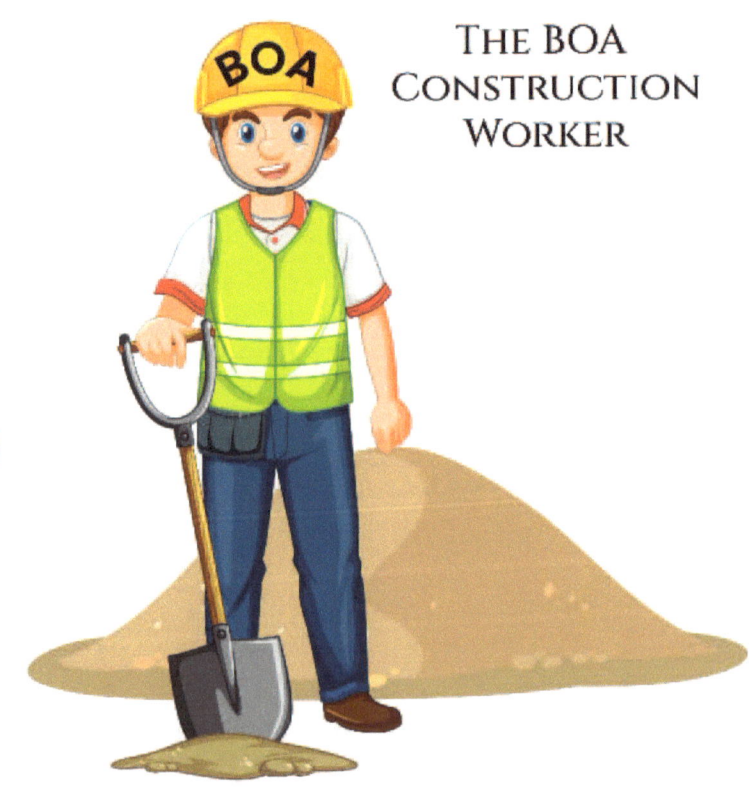

THE BOA
CONSTRUCTION
WORKER

What Creature keeps the drinks cold in the Swamp?

RefridgeiGATOR

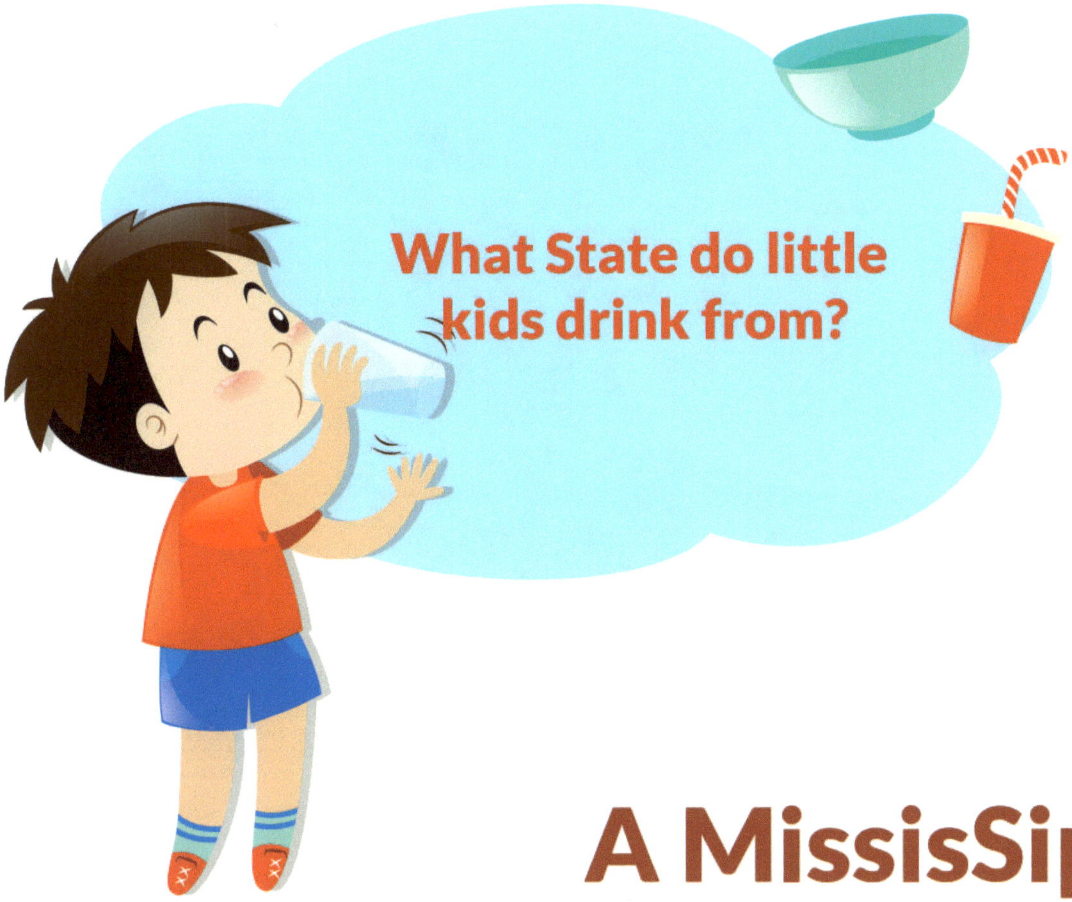
What State do little kids drink from?

A MissisSippi Cup

MISSIS
SIPPI

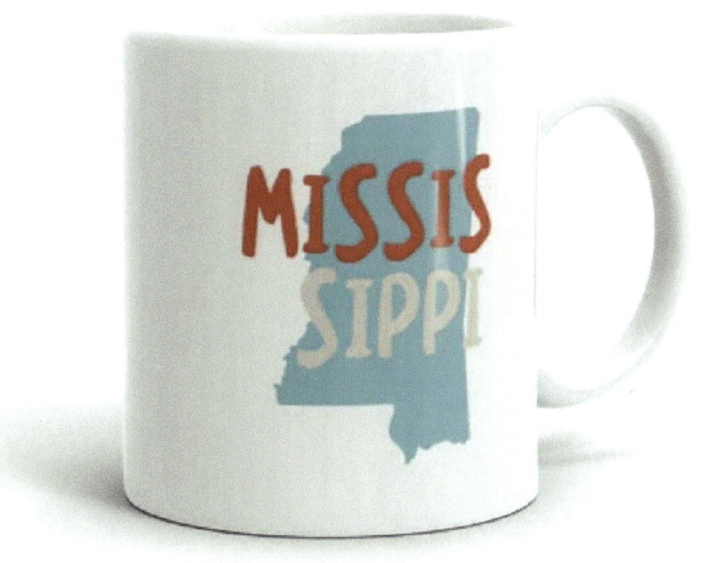

What insects help fight body ordor?

DeodorANTS

What do you call 100 Ballerinas all in a line?

A TU TU TRAIN

When do Crabs get mad?

When they are
STEAMED

HOW DO YOU GET HAY OUT OF JAIL?

PAY IT'S BALE

WHO DO YOU CALL WHEN THE QUEEN OF HEARTS HAS A HEART ATTACK?

CARDiologist.

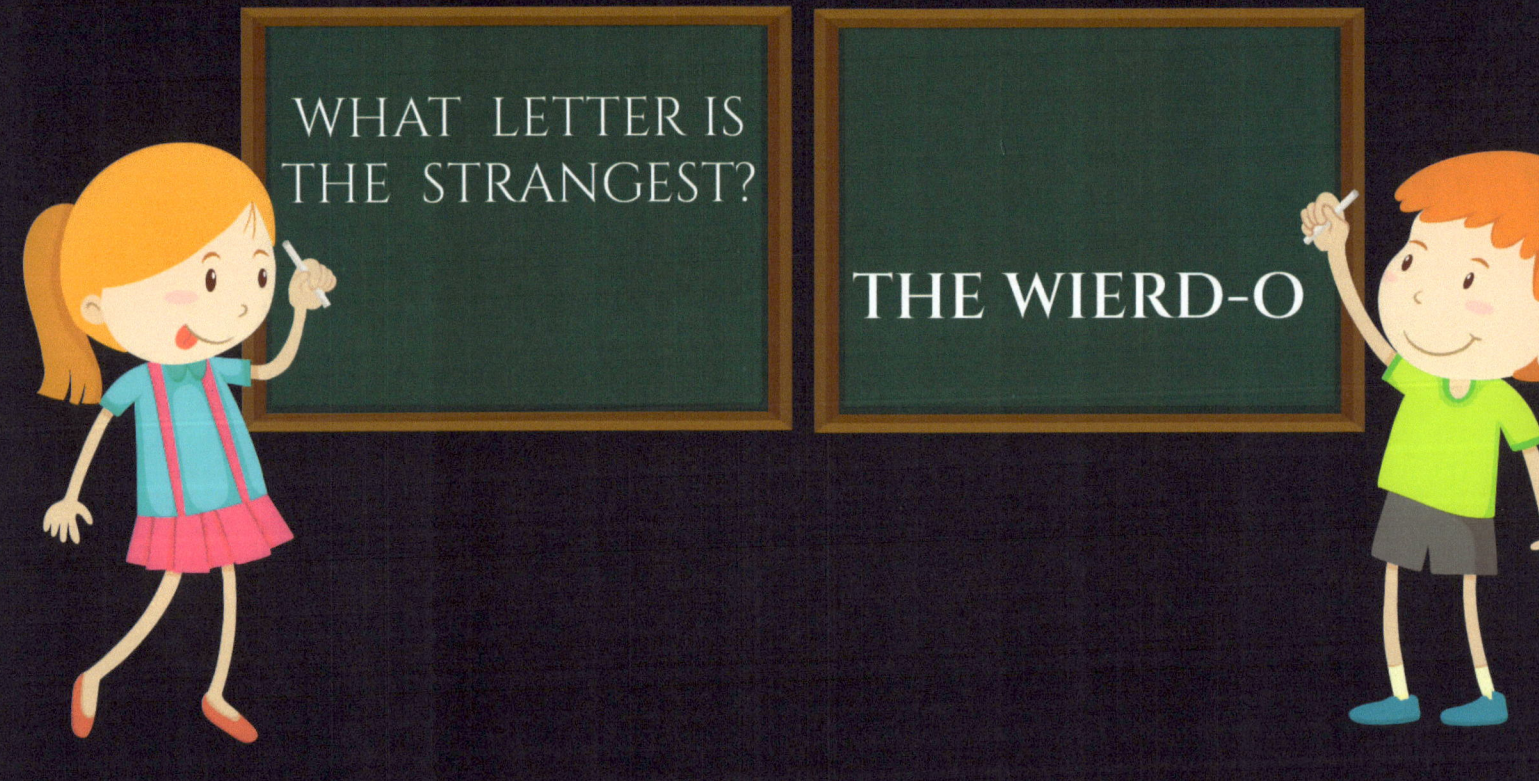

WHAT LETTER IS THE STRANGEST?

THE WIERD-O

WHAT SEA CREATURE ALWAYS SCORES A RINGER?

THE HORSESHOE CRAB

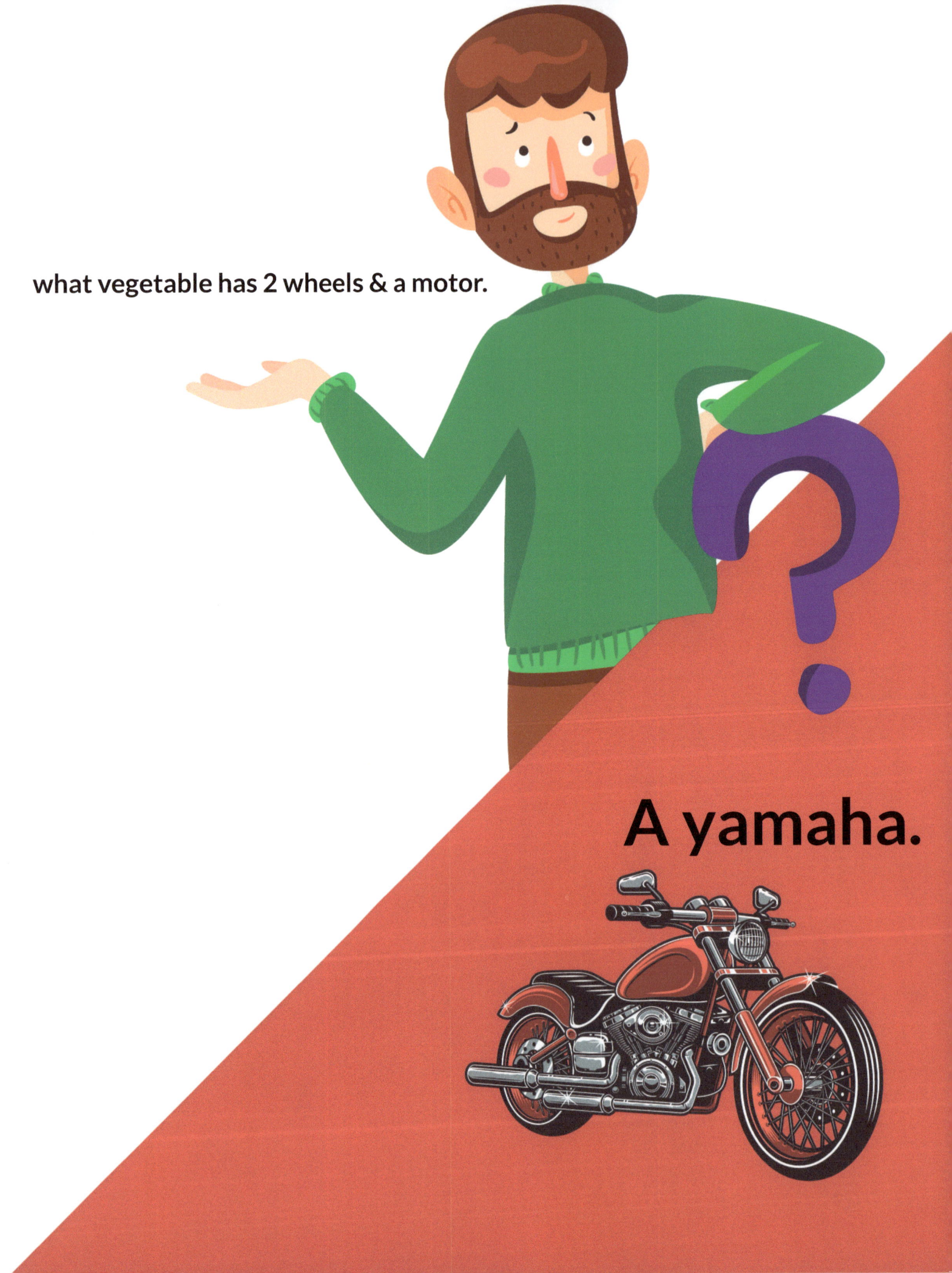

WHAT MUSICAL INSTRUMENT DO DOGS PREFER?

tromBONE

WHAT SUBJECT DO SNAKES TEACH?

HISSTORY

HOW DO ESKAMOES KEEP THEIR HOUSES TOGETHER?

WITH IGLUE

WHAT TREE
LOVES TO TALK?

THE SPEACH TREE

WHAT DOES THE QUEEN BEE WEAR TO THE BEACH?

HER BEEKEENEE

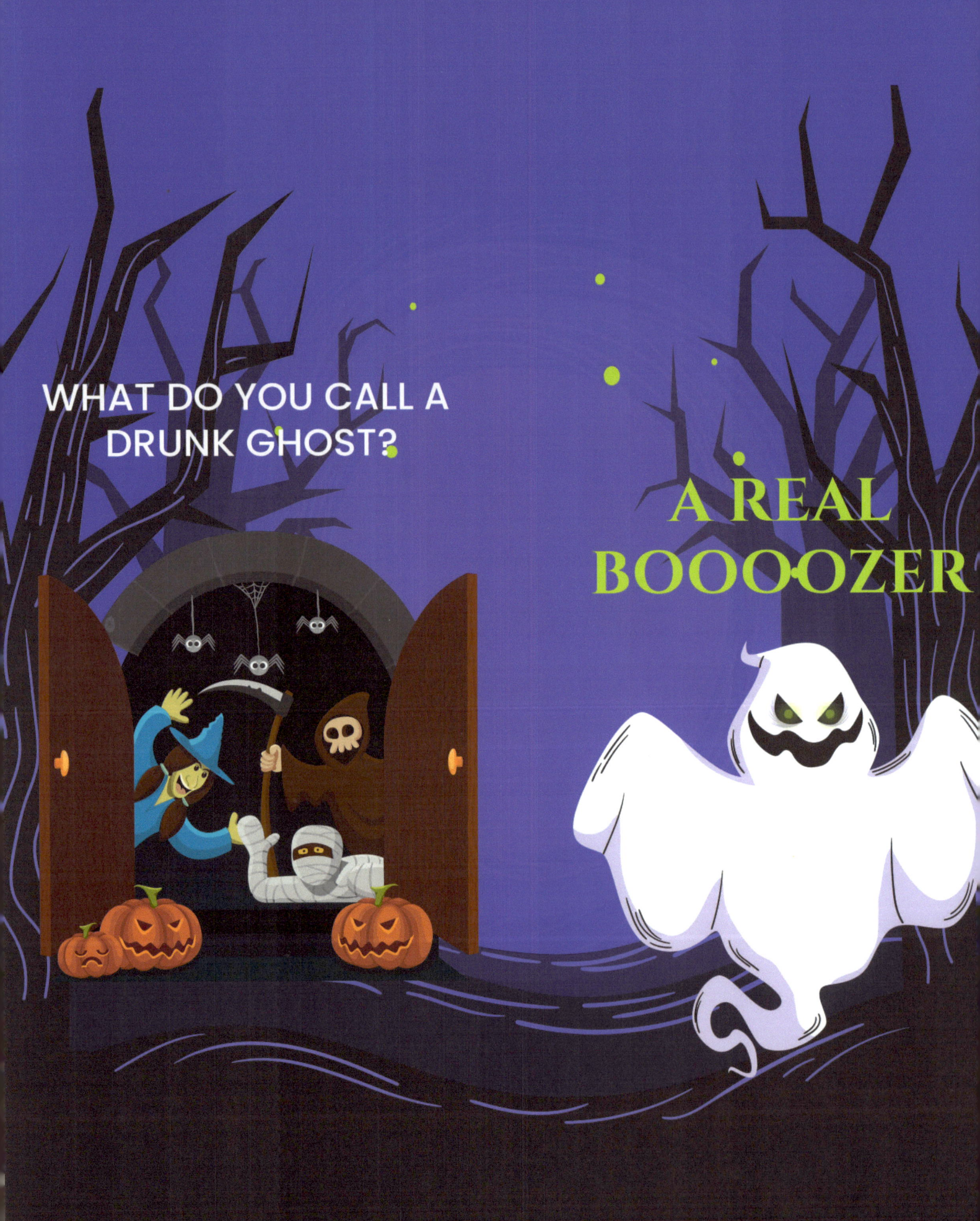

How do you groom a Rabbit?

WITH A HAREBRUSH

What do you call a Rabbit in Heaven?

AN ANGELHARE

WHAT DO SHIPS EAT FOR BREAKFAST?

BOATMEAL

WHAT FISH IS THE FUNNIEST?

THE CLOWN FIS

WHAT COLOR WOULD A BELCH BE?

BURPPLE

WHAT ANIMAL NEVER TELLS THE TRUTH?

THE LION

WHAT CREATURE IS A TRUE FLOWERCHILD?

THE HIPPYPOTAMUS

NEVER INVITE THIS CAT TO PLAY POKER?

HE IS A CHEETAH

WHAT KITCHEN UTINSEL
IS THE MEANEST?

THE EGG BEATER

SANTA SENT RUDOLPH TO SCHOOL

NOW HE IS A BRAINDEER

WHERE DO WOUNDED
JOCKEYS GO?

THE HORSEPITAL

WHAT DID THE SEA SEE
WHEN IT SAW WHAT IT SAW?

The Sea saw
what IT was Looking AT

WHAT MUSICAL INSTRUMENT SWIMS IN THE OCEAN?

THE STUBADIVER

WHAT BIRD SKATES ON THE ICE?

THE HAWKY PLAYER

What do you get when you cross a Stick with Dracula?

A baseball BAT

How do Cows get from one Town to another?

How does William TELL stay in shape

ARROWbics

AEROBICS

What condiment scares Mice?

CATsup

WHAT SNAKE DIRECTS AN ORCHASTRA?

THE **BOA**CONDUCTOR

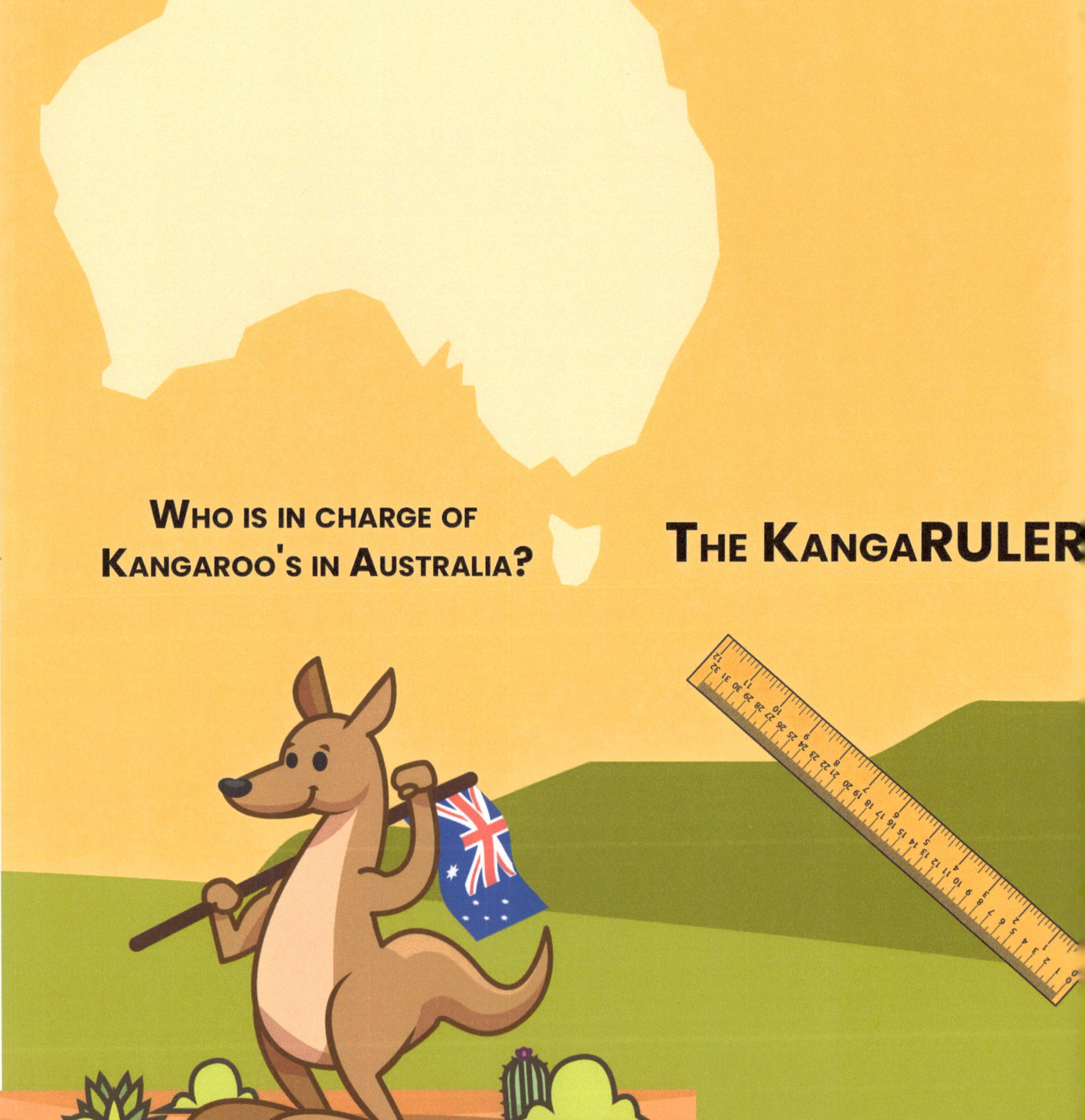

WHERE DO BANDIT BEES GO AFTER A RAID?

THEIR HIVEOUT

HOW CAN YOU TELL THAT A COW IS FROM HAWAII?

IT WEARS A MUU MUU

What music style do birds enjoy?

SWING

NASA should offer a training Course for those who don't want to go into Space.

AstroNOTS101

Why are Golf Balls so cute?

They have DIMPLES

It couln't get the LEAD out.

Why did the Pencil lose
it's race with the Pen?

WIRE WE HERE

What did one telephone pole ask the other?

Commercials have
sure changed,

today they should
be called CONmericial

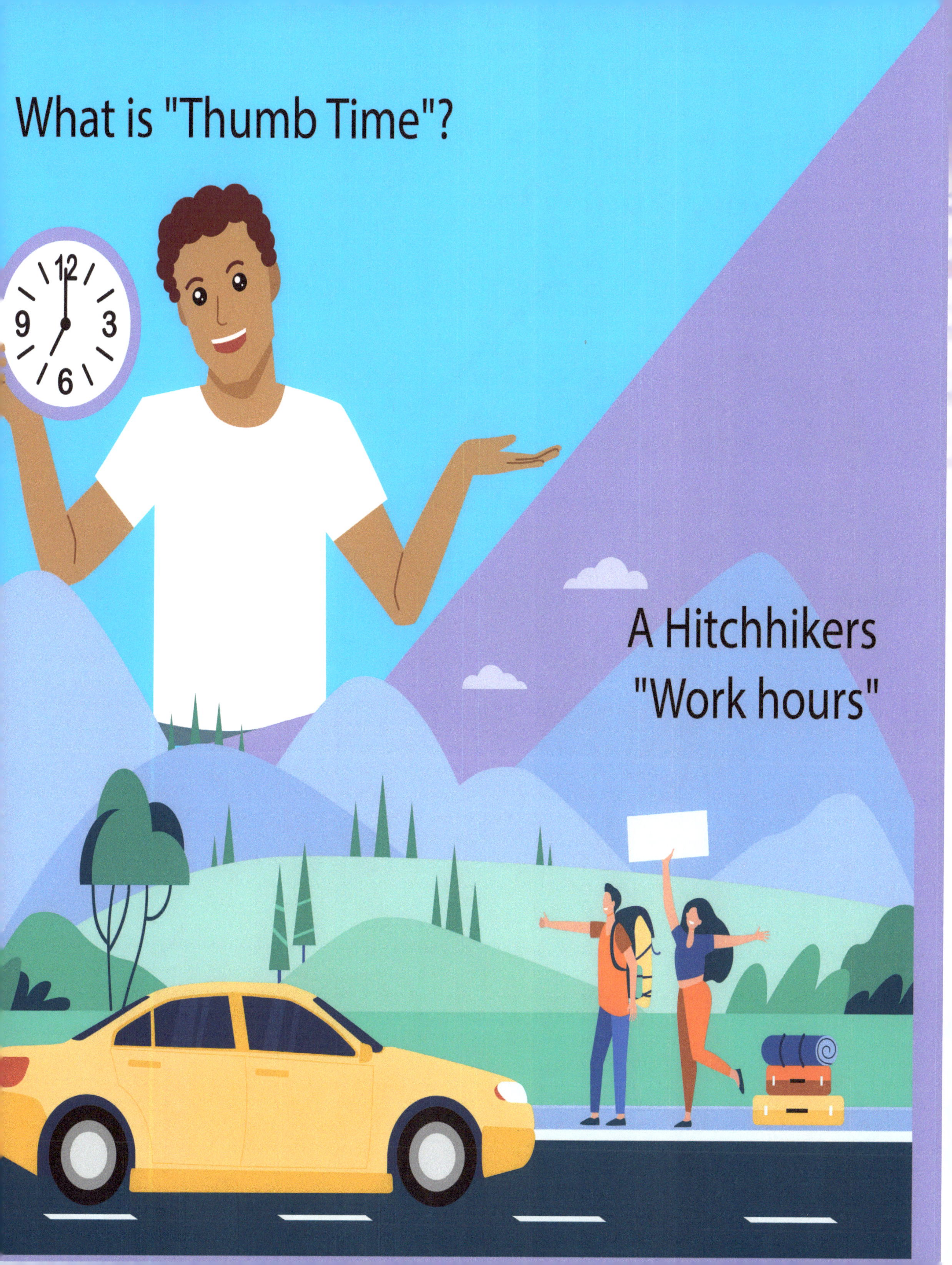
What is "Thumb Time"?
12
3
6
9
A Hitchhikers
"Work hours"

What kind of BEE is very clumsy?

THE FUMBLE BEE

Why did the car hire a Writer?

To write it's AUTObiography

What insect spins through the air

A FrisBEE

What insect says "Grace" at dinertime?

The Praying Mantis

What insect is only part of a foot?

The MosquiTOE

What do you put on
a Hot Sled Dog?

MUSHterd

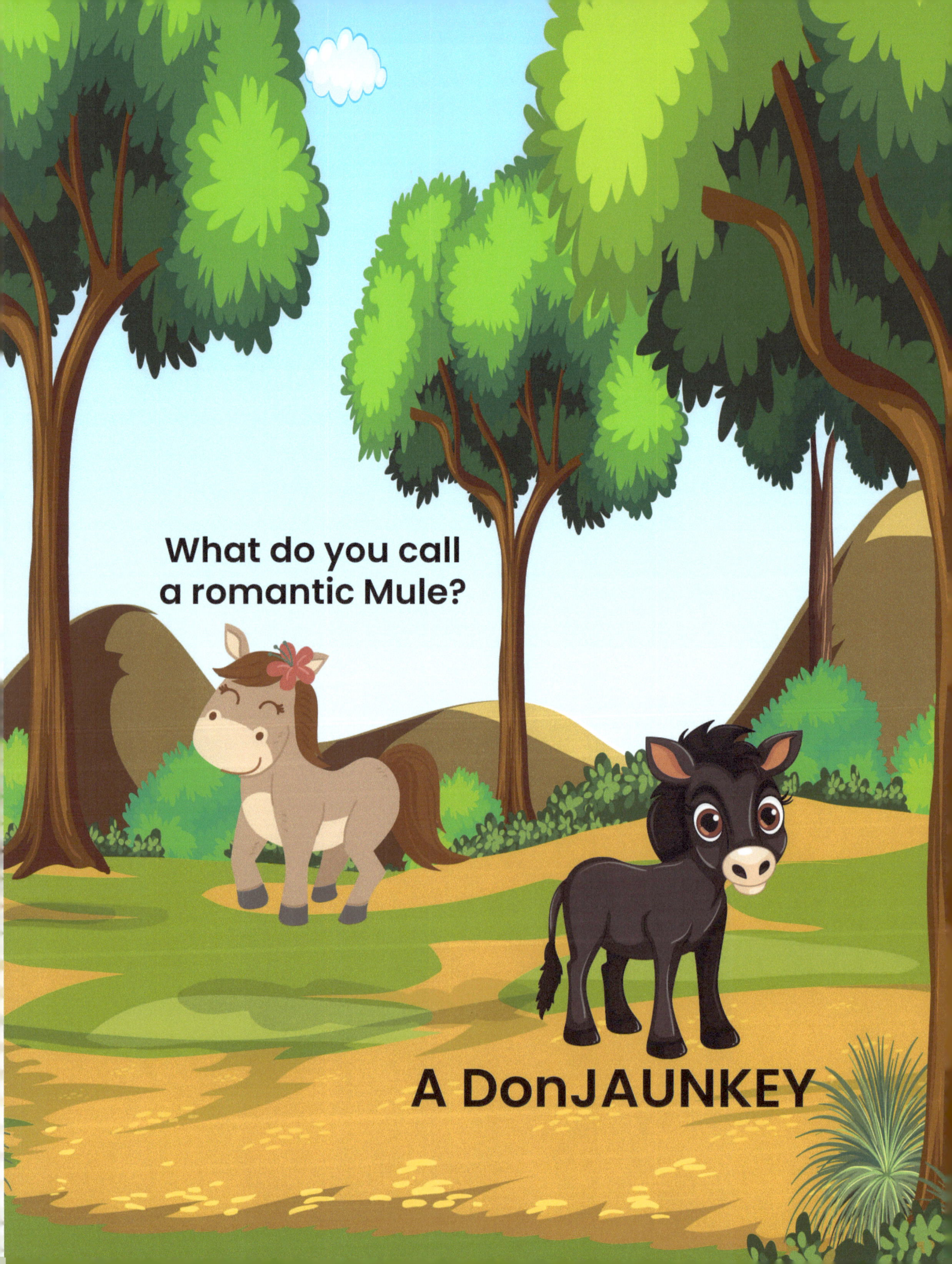

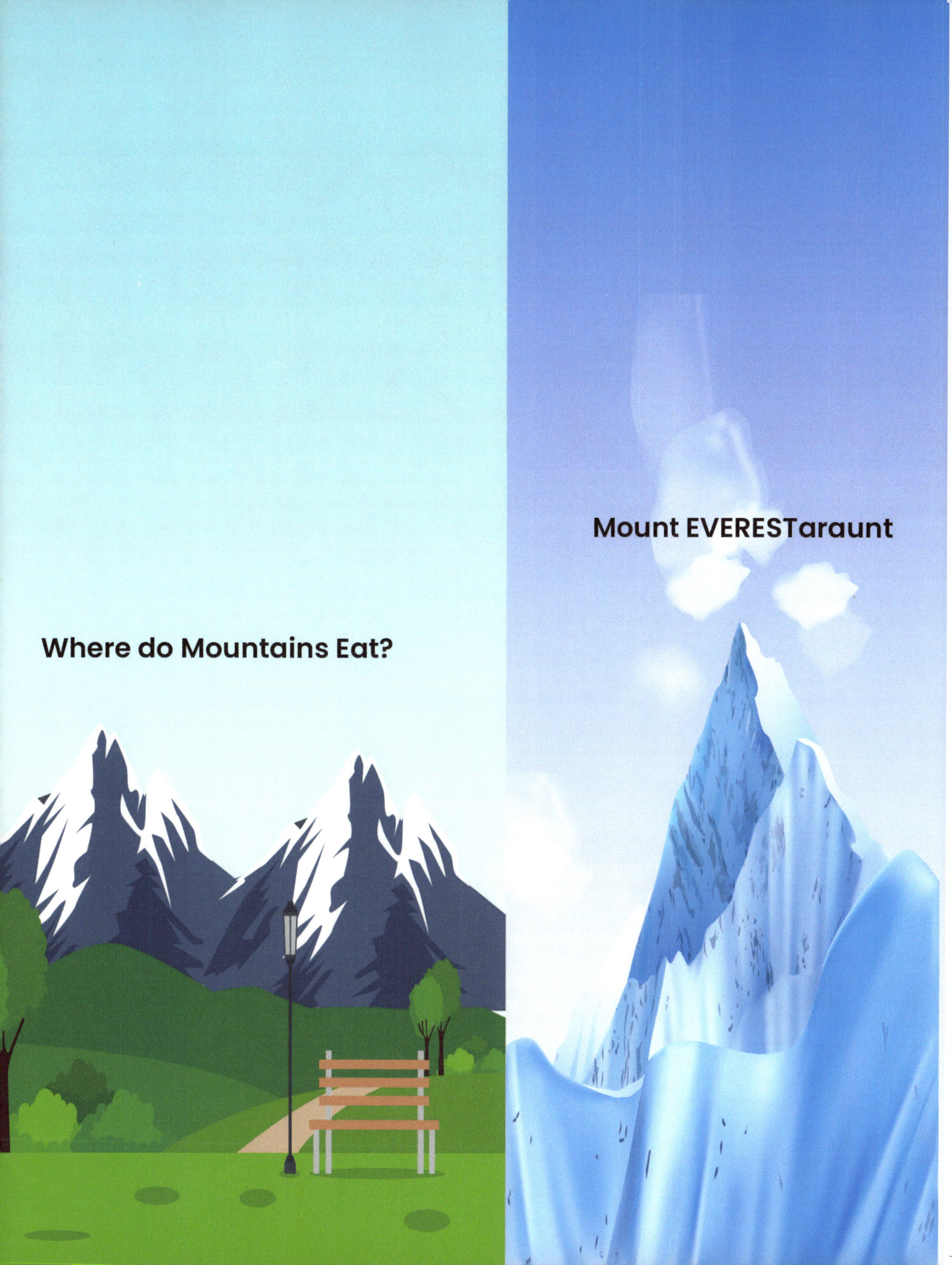

Where do Mountains Eat?

Mount EVERESTaraunt

Why do the Critters go into the Woods?

ForREST

Where do Skunks do their dishes?

IN A STINK

What Car can you fold?

The Mercedes BENDS

What pooch works in an office?

A SECRATERRIE

What Reptile is best suited for Policework?

The InvestiGATOR

What do you call a Tree that just doesn't get it?

STUMPED

What would Shakespear call his new musical?

TUBA or not TUBA

.What do you serve at a
Cats Birthday Party?

Cake and MICEcream

What kind of Slipper does Bread prefer?

LOAFers

What does a Drunk use to clean his Ears?

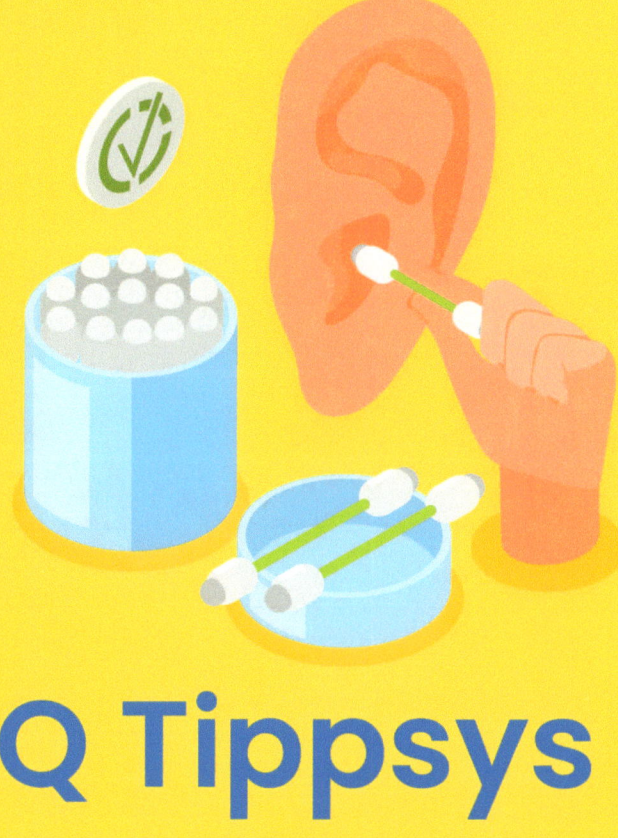

Q Tippsys

Does Frosty the Snowman sneeze.

Who sNOse

What Food always makes you smile.

Cheese

What fish swims in Reverse?

BASSACKWARD

Milk of AMNESIA

What do forgetful people drink with dinner?

What Fruit is never Happy?

The CRABapple

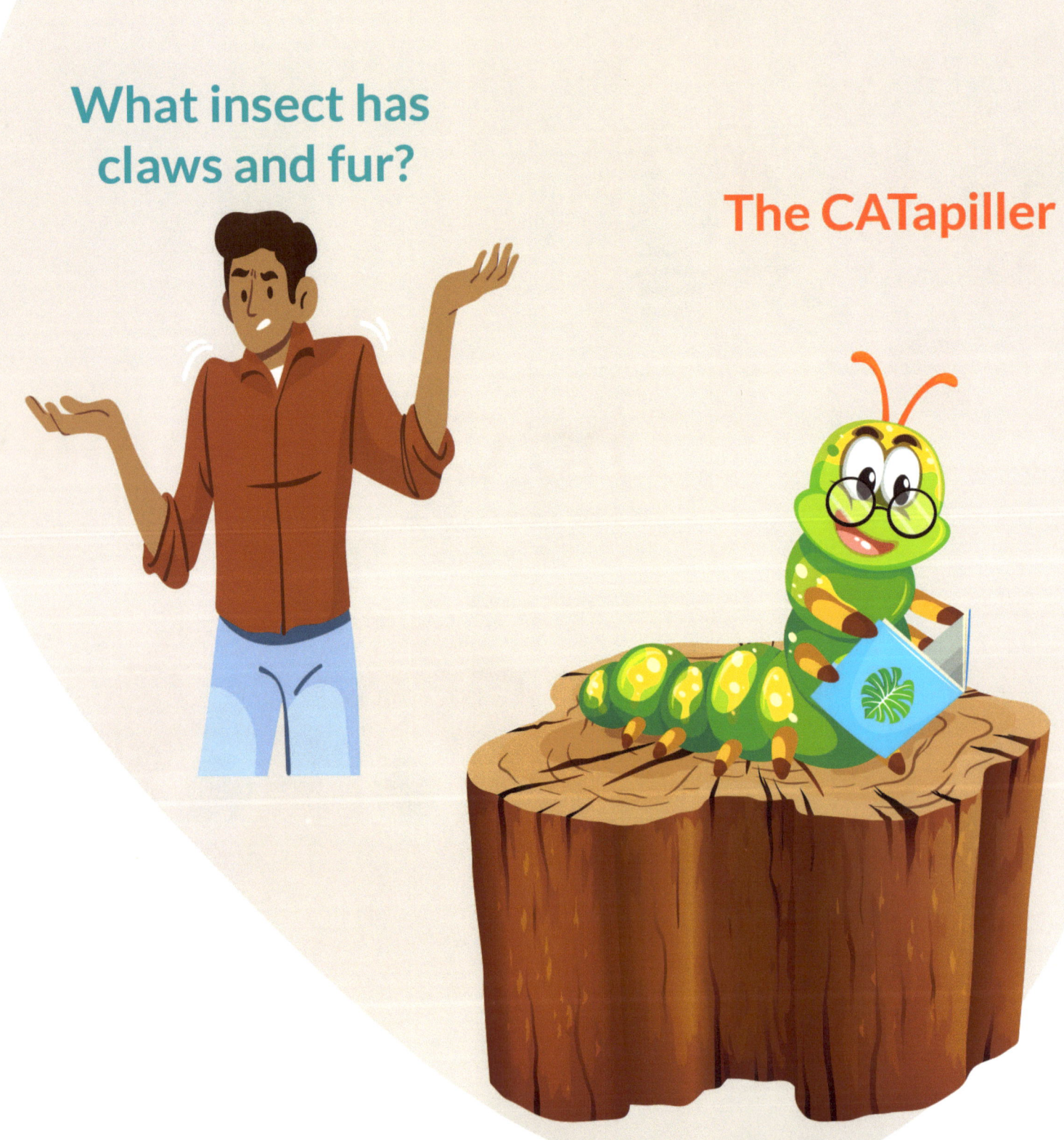

What kind of Moustache
do you find on a Mountain?

MOUNTAIN GOATEE

What do you call a sleepy Bull?

A BullDOZER

What Fish is a Carpenters Tool?

The
HAMMERHEAD
shark

What Bird can you find sitting at the Bar

A STOOL Pigeon?

?

WHAT DO YOU GET WHEN YOU CROSS A FANCY CAT AND A FLOWER?

A DANDYLION

What do you get when you cross a Truck and a Frog?

JUMPING TRUCK

What insect pesters Clocks?

TICs

What is a BLIND tree's best friend?

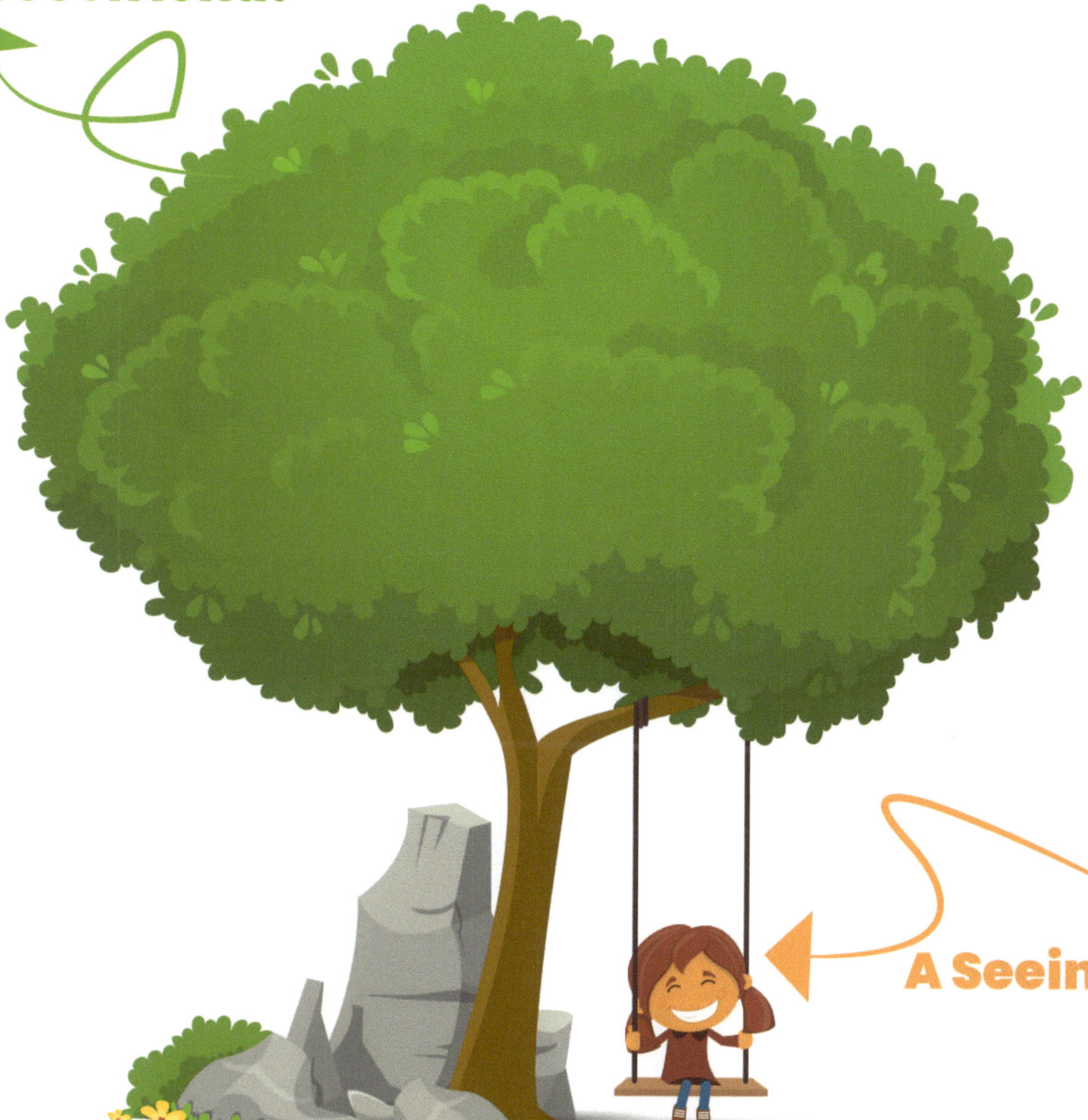

A Seeing eye LOG

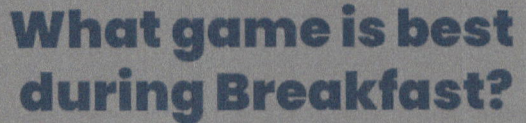

What game is best during Breakfast?

SCRABBLED EGGS

What do you call a Crazy Spaceman?

An AstroNUT

Where do the 3 Musketeers enjoy their Beers?

At a CandyBAR

What Bird never needs a Haircut?

The Bald Eagle

What do Clocks read?

Time Magizine

What Bird can write letters?

THE SPEELICAN

What School has the best Swimmers?

A School of Fish

Four SECONDS

Why do Clocks go back at Dinnertime?

WHAT STATE HAS THE MOST PLASTIC SURGEONS?

SKIN-TUCKY

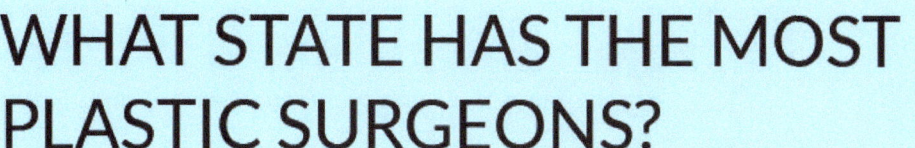

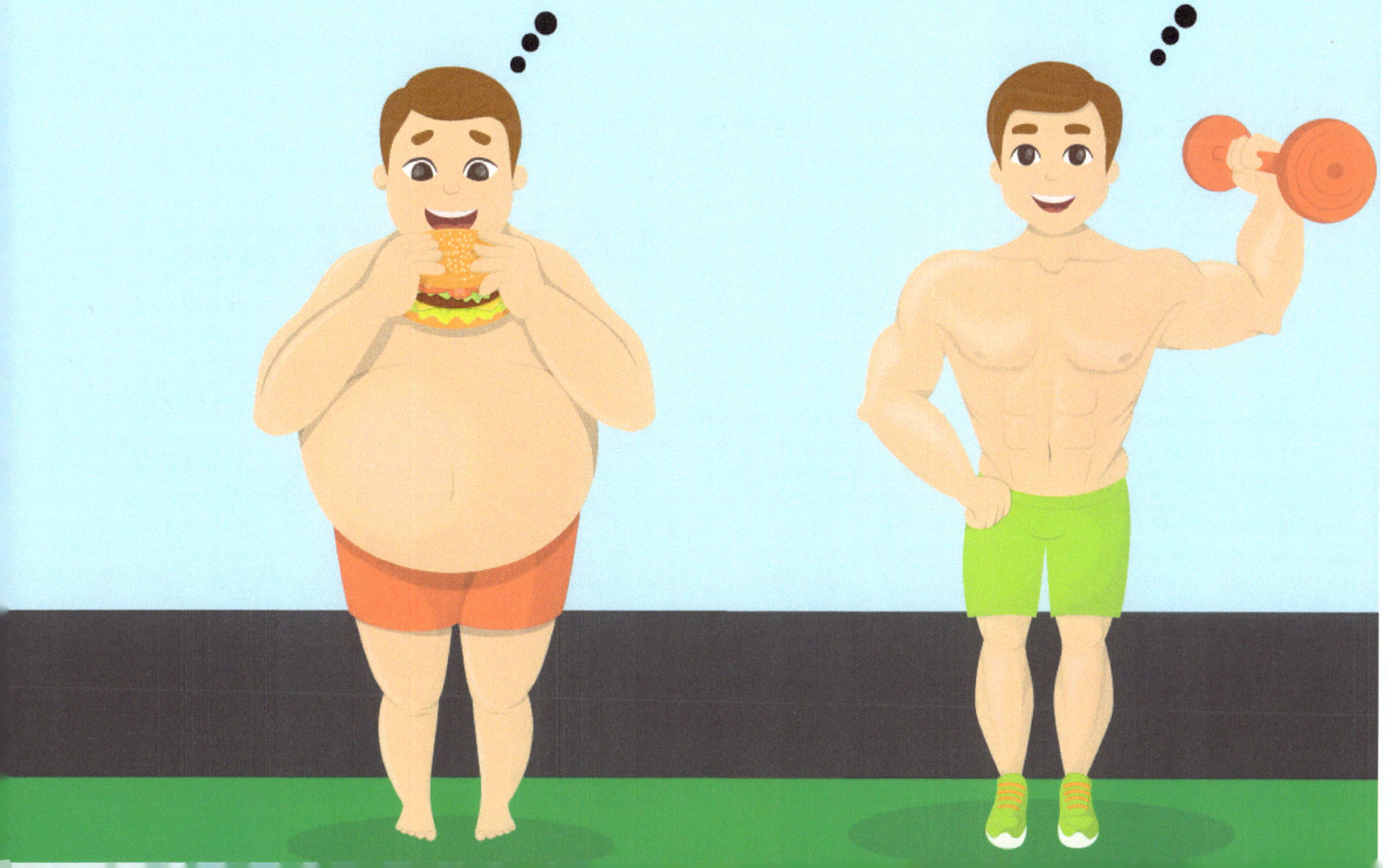

What car do wealthy Sheep drive?

LAMBorgenees

Did you hear about the Poor Wolf ?

Known as the Wolf in
cheap Clothing.

What Car does Music prefer?

A Rock and Rollsroyce

WHAT VEHICLES ARE EDIBLE?

BIG MAC TRUCKS

What do Ants look-up to?

Everything

Why can't you hide anything from a Mountain?

Because they always PEAK

WHAT BIRD NEVER LOSSES IT'S HEAD?

A DUCK

What Car do Cows prefer?
CATTLEac

What do you call a Beatles pet rabbit?
A BUGS BUNNY

**What Musical instrument does a Grizzly play?
The BEARatone**

What instrument do Pants play?
The SLACKSaphone

What insect is always undercover?
The SPYder

What do Planets Snack on?
MoonPies

**What do you call a Drunk Ghost?
A real BOOOOzer**

Where do BullFighters shop?
At the sTORO sTORO

Where does the smallest puppy eat?
In a RestaRUNT

What do you do after you crash your Car? Perform an AUTOtopsy

Where do Alaskans keep their Pigs?
In PigLoos

What State has a school for Cows?
MOOOtah

What is it called when Concrete gets together for Drinks?
A CEMENTmixer

What Nut is always Sneezing?
The cASHEW

What is an Eskimoes favorite Mexican Dish?
The BURRRRRito

Where do Baby Pigs go?
NewHAMshire

Where do Baby Frogs sleep?
In cRIBBITS

What Bike does a Rancher ride?
A COWasaki

What is another name for a Barn?
A COWdominium

How does a Plumber get around?
On a RotoSCOOTER

What letter holds lots of fish?
C

what do you get when you cross a
bird and a pair of shoes?
A Paracleats

What does Dracula never order at a restaurant?
Stake

What Veggie can you sell again?
ReCelery

What Meal is not eaten today?
StewMorrow

Where do Dogs stay
when they go to College?
A LABRADORmatory

What was the Corn arrested for?
Stalking

What happens when water trips?
Waterfalls

What Sea Creature is a great actor?
The MovieSTARFISH

What River can not remember where it's going?
The seeNILE

What animal is a Streaker?
The in the BUFFallo

What are the Doctors and Nurses doing in the Delivery Room?
Having a LABOR Party

What Mystic studies Trees?
A PALM reader

What kind of Rash do houses suffer with?
Shingles

Why couldn't the Shoe play in the Band?
It had no ShoeHORN

What Bear is just too cute?
The Pandorable Bear

Where does a Bull take his date?
To the MOOvies

What Flower only opens part-way?
The Lazy Dazy

What Letter dirinks to much?
The WineO

What staircase is never early?
An EscaLATER

What do you call a Log in front of a Turtle?
A Turdle Hurdle

What can you tell a stubborn Sheep?
Mutton

Why did the Penny cry?
It was CENTimental